ASTERIX AND THE GOLDEN SICKLE

TEXT BY GOSCINNY

DRAWINGS BY UDERZO

TRANSLATED BY ANTHEA BELL AND DEREK HOCKRIDGE

HODDER DARGAUD
LONDON SYDNEY AUCKLAND

Asterix and the Golden Sickle
Copyright © Dargaud Editeur 1962, Goscinny-Uderzo
English language text copyright © Hodder and Stoughton Ltd 1975

ISBN 0-340-41025-6

This omnibus edition first published 1987

Published by Hodder Dargaud Ltd,
Mill Road, Dunton Green, Sevenoaks, Kent TN13 2YJ

Printed in Belgium by Henri Proost et Cie, Turnhout

GAULISH VILLAGE

COMPENDIUM

LAUDANUM

AQUARIUM

TOTORUM

ARMORICA

BELGICA

LUTETIA

SPQR

GAUL
(ROMAN CONQUEST)
50 B.C.

CELTICA

PROVINCIA

AQUITANIA

he year is 50 BC. Gaul is entirely occupied by the Romans.
Vell, not entirely… One small village of indomitable Gauls still
olds out against the invaders. And life is not easy for the
oman legionaries who garrison the fortified camps of
otorum, Aquarium, Laudanum and Compendium…

a few of the Gauls

Asterix, the hero of these adventures. A shrewd, cunning little warrior; all perilous missions are immediately entrusted to him. Asterix gets his superhuman strength from the magic potion brewed by the druid Getafix...

Obelix, Asterix's inseparable friend. A menhir delivery-man by trade; addicted to wild boar. Obelix is always ready to drop everything and go off on a new adventure with Asterix – so long as there's wild boar to eat, and plenty of fighting.

Getafix, the venerable village druid. Gathers mistletoe and brews magic potions. His speciality is the potion which gives the drinker superhuman strength. But Getafix also has other recipes up his sleeve...

Cacofonix, the bard. Opinion is divided as to his musical gifts. Cacofonix thinks he's a genius. Everyone else thinks he's unspeakable. But so long as he doesn't speak, let alone sing, everybody likes him...

Finally, Vitalstatistix, the chief of the tribe. Majestic, brave and hot-tempered, the old warrior is respected by his men and feared by his enemies. Vitalstatistix himself has only one fear; he is afraid the sky may fall on his head tomorrow. But as he always says, 'Tomorrow never comes.'

Asterix and the Golden Sickle

THE FIERCELY INDEPENDENT LITTLE VILLAGE WHERE ASTERIX AND THE OTHER GAULS LIVE IS AT PEACE...

GOOD HUNTING, ASTERIX?

NOTHING MUCH TODAY...

OBELIX IS HAPPILY AT WORK, CARVING OUT A MENHIR ...

THERE'LL ALWAYS BE A GAU-AAH!...

CACOFONIX THE BARD IS GIVING THE CHILDREN LESSONS...

WELL, YOUNG MAN, AND INTO HOW MANY PARTS IS GAUL DIVIDED?

$VIII \times V = XL$

$\dfrac{\begin{array}{r} III \\ + I \end{array}}{= IV}$

?

IN SHORT, EVERYONE IS CONTENTED. ALL IS PEACE AND PLENTY ...

ANOTHER BOAR, OBELIX?

YES, PLEASE!

WHEN SUDDENLY ...

OH, BY TOUTATIS!

?

??

?

?

WHAT'S ALL THAT SHOUTING?

IT'S THE VOICE OF OUR DRUID GETAFIX!

IT'S COMING FROM THAT OAK TREE OVER THERE!

SCRGNGNGNONRR... ARCHRGHGHN... GNEUGNEU...

WHAT'S THE MATTER, O DRUID?

BY BELENOS, TOUTATIS AND BELISAMA! I'VE BROKEN MY GOLDEN SICKLE!

THIS IS TERRIBLE! MISTLETOE MUST BE CUT WITH A GOLDEN SICKLE IF IT IS TO HAVE MAGIC POWERS!

IT COULDN'T BE WORSE TIMED! I HAVE TO START SOON FOR THE FOREST OF THE CARNUTES, TO ATTEND THE GREAT ANNUAL CONFERENCE OF GAULISH DRUIDS. I CAN'T GO WITHOUT A SICKLE!

ALL YOU HAVE TO DO IS BUY ANOTHER ONE!

GOOD SICKLES DON'T GROW ON TREES!

THE BEST, INDEED THE ONLY ONES I CONSIDER WORTH USING, ARE MADE BY THE FAMOUS METALLURGIX, IN FARAWAY LUTETIA...

HE'S RIGHT. IT'S WELL KNOWN THAT METALLURGIX MAKES THE BEST SICKLES...

YOU'RE RIGHT THERE...

AND LUTETIA IS A LONG WAY OFF... YOU HAVE TO PASS THROUGH FORESTS FULL OF BARBARIANS AND BANDITS TO GET THERE!

I AM PREPARED TO GO TO LUTETIA, O DRUID!

7

NIGHT IS FALLING, OBELIX. THERE'S AN INN NEAR HERE CALLED THE CONTRITE BARBARIAN. WE'LL STOP THERE!!!

DANGER
SLIPPERY FLAGSTONES

THIS INN IS FAMOUS FOR ITS SPECIALITY: ROAST BOAR!

ROAST OR JUST SERVED RAW AS A SIMPLE LITTLE SALAD, BOAR IS MY FAVOURITE FOOD!

Velcome! You vant a room?

THAT'S RIGHT. AND TWO BOARS.

TWO FOR ME TOO!

YOU CAN TAKE OUR LUGGAGE TO OUR ROOM.

???

Und vhere are you going like zat?

TO LUTETIA!!!

SCRUNCH! SCRUNCH! SCRUNCH!

Aaah! Ludetia!

I'VE JUST COME FROM LUTETIA!!!

HAVE YOU?

A BEAUTIFUL CITY, LUTETIA, BUT DANGEROUS, VERY DANGEROUS!

OH, COME! WE'RE ONLY GOING THERE TO BUY A SICKLE.

A SICKLE? SICKLES ARE IN SHORT SUPPLY IN LUTETIA JUST NOW.

DON'T WORRY, WE KNOW WHERE TO GO!

NEXT MORNING...

Auf wiedersehen!

The Coul Barbar

HEY, ASTERIX, WHY DO YOU THINK THAT TRAVELLER TOLD US SICKLES WERE IN SHORT SUPPLY IN LUTETIA?

NO IDEA, OBELIX.

LET'S ENJOY OUR JOURNEY; WE CAN WORRY ABOUT THAT LATER...

THE ROMANS ARE RUINING THE LANDSCAPE WITH ALL THESE MODERN BUILDINGS!

OUR FRIENDS' JOURNEY PROCEEDS WITHOUT MUCH INCIDENT, APART FROM A FEW SCUFFLES WITH BANDITS...

AT SUINDINUM, ASTERIX AND OBELIX ARE UNABLE TO FIND A BED, AS IT HAPPENS TO BE THE DAY OF THE GREAT OX-CART RACE, THE SUINDINUM 24 HOURS...

BUT AT LAST, ONE DAY...

LOOK! OBELIX!

LUTETIA!

ISN'T IT BIG!

WHAT A LOT OF PEOPLE! FANCY LIVING HERE! TALK ABOUT POLLUTION!

LET'S FIND METALLURGIX'S HOUSE AS FAST AS WE CAN!

OUT OF THE WAY THERE, BARBARIAN!

WHO DO YOU THINK YOU ARE, BEN HUR?

WE'LL ASK THAT FISHERMAN. HE DOESN'T LOOK TOO BUSY.

ARE THEY BITING?

WHAT WITH ALL THE MUCK PEOPLE ARE THROWING INTO THE RIVER, THERE AREN'T ANY FISH LEFT. I'VE CAUGHT NOTHING BUT EMPTY AMPHORAS ALL MORNING.

DO YOU KNOW THE WAY TO METALLURGIX'S HOUSE, PLEASE?

THE SICKLE DEALER? THIRD ON THE RIGHT.

METALLURGIX SICKLES
DRUIDS SPECIALLY CATERED FOR
LATEST LUTETIA FASHIONS
ANTIQUES

WHAT DO YOU WANT?

I'VE COME TO WARN YOU THERE ARE TWO MEN LOOKING FOR METALLURGIX.

METALLURGIX? WELL, WELL... AND WHAT ARE THESE MEN LIKE?

NO SPECIAL DISTINGUISHING MARKS. A FAT GAUL AND A LITTLE GAUL.

OH YES, I FORGOT. ONE OF THEM CARRIES A MENHIR ABOUT WITH HIM.

A MENHIR?

RIGHT. CLEAR OFF, AND KEEP YOUR MOUTH SHUT IF YOU WANT TO STAY ALIVE!

DON'T WORRY. I'LL BE DUMB AS A DOLMEN!

NOW TO TRY AND FIND THOSE TWO NOSEY PARKERS...

10.A

BY BELENOS, I THINK I'M IN LUCK!

THIS IS SERIOUS. IF OUR DRUID IS TO ATTEND THE CONFERENCE IN THE FOREST OF THE CARNUTES WE MUST GET HOLD OF A SICKLE FOR HIM. IT'S URGENT!

AND WE MUST GET HOLD OF A BOAR FOR ME. THAT'S URGENT TOO...

YOU MAKE ME SICK, GOING ON ABOUT BOARS ALL THE TIME!

AND YOU BORE ME GOING ON ABOUT SICKLES!

10.B

SO SORRY. HOW CLUMSY OF ME!

DON'T MENTION IT!

IT WAS NOTHING!

YOU LOOK LIKE STRANGERS TO OUR GREAT CITY. PERHAPS I CAN HELP YOU?

WE'RE LOOKING FOR METALLURGIX....

METALLURGIX? WHY HE'S MY BEST FRIEND! AND WHAT DO YOU WANT HIM FOR?

WHAT A LUCKY COINCIDENCE!

WE WANT TO BUY A GOLDEN SICKLE FROM HIM.

EXCELLENT, EXCELLENT!

METALLURGIX HAS RETIRED AND LEFT LUTETIA.

OH DEAR!

BUT NEVER MIND. YOU COME WITH ME. I CAN GET YOU A SICKLE AT A VERY COMPETITIVE PRICE!

WELL, THE THING IS...

AND WHAT AM I GOING TO DO WITH MY MENHIR?

WOULD YOU LIKE TO LEAVE YOUR THINGS?

CLOAKS

15

THE SUN, RISING ON LUTETIA, IS GREETED BY A COCKEREL...

COCK-A-DOODLE-DO!

GET UP, OBELIX! IT'S TIME TO START OUR INVESTIGATIONS!

THAT'S RIGHT. WE MUST FIND METALLURGIX.

LET'S GO BACK TO THAT ARVERNIAN IN THE WINE SHOP. I'M SURE HE KNOWS SOMETHING!

THE SUN OF MASSILIA

OH!

COULD YOU TELL US WHERE TO FIND THE ARVERNIAN WHO...

OH, I EXPECT YOU MEAN THE FORMER PROPRIETOR?

THAT CRAZY GAUL WHO SOLD ME THIS PLACE FOR A HANDFUL OF BRONZE COINS! IT'S UNDER NEW MANAGEMENT NOW, BUT YOU WON'T BE DISAPPOINTED!

I CAN OFFER YOU MY SPECIALITY: FISH SOUP! MADE OF NICE FRESH FISH, JUST ARRIVED BY OX-CART FROM MASSILIA!

DO YOU KNOW WHERE THE ARVERNIAN HAS GONE?

OH! HE STARTED FOR GERGOVIA THIS MORNING, TRAVELLING BY OX-CART, THE SAME AS THE FISH!

THE SUN OF MASSILIA

WHAT A SHAME! IF YOU'D COME A LITTLE SOONER YOU'D HAVE FOUND HIM STILL HERE!

THANKS!

ALL THESE LUTETIANS ARE CRAZY, BY BELISAMA!

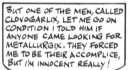

WE MUST FIND THE DOLMEN WHERE CLOVOGARLIX AND NAVISHTRIX MEET!

IT WON'T BE EASY...

YOU NEVER KNOW. THE LUTETIANS CAN'T HAVE MANY DOLMENS ...

POOR THINGS!

WE SHOULD BE ABLE TO GET SOME INFORMATION OVER THERE ...

visit Lutetia

CLAUDIUS OMNIBUS, GUIDE

LATIN SPOKEN
CELTIC SPOKEN
Gothic Spoken

DO YOU WANT TO SEE OUR BEAUTIFUL CITY?

NO, WE WANT TO SEE SOME DOLMENS!

LUTETIA NIGHTS

ILLUMINATIONS
AMUSEMENTS
GAIETY
3 SESTERTII

WE HAVEN'T ANY DOLMENS AROUND HERE!

(SIGH) POOR THINGS!

SURELY THERE MUST BE AT LEAST ONE!

JUST A MINUTE ... NOW I COME TO THINK OF IT, I HAVE HEARD OF A DOLMEN IN THE FOREST... THE FOREST OVER WHERE THE SUN SETS ...

JUST THE JOB! TAKE US TO THAT FOREST!

NO! THERE ARE WOLVES AND BANDITS IN THAT FOREST!

WOULDN'T YOU RATHER SEE A SHOW AT THE FAMOUS MOLA RUBRA? 3 SESTERTII AND AS MUCH BEER AS YOU CAN DRINK!

NO, THANK YOU!

LET'S GO AND FIND THAT FOREST OVER WHERE THE SUN SETS!

ONE SINGLE, SOLITARY DOLMEN ... POOR THINGS!

visit Lutetia

24

13.60

WARM RAYS OF BRILLIANT SUNSHINE LIGHT UP A CLOUDLESS SKY...

... LITTLE BIRDS WARBLE ON THE LEAFY BRANCHES ...

... SQUIRRELS PLAY ON THE MOSSY GROUND ...

... WHILE UNDERNEATH THE MOSSY GROUND....

BOING!

PLAF!

OUCH!

EEEEH

GET THEM OBELIX!

YOU BET I WILL, ASTERIX!

BOUM!

BONG! BONG!

BONG!

ARE THERE ANY LEFT, ASTERIX?

NO, OBELIX, YOU'RE JUST FINISHING OFF THE LAST ONE...

LET'S GET OUT OF HERE AND WARN THE BOSS!

OBELIX, I'M A BIT WORRIED... I CAN'T FIND NANISHTRIX!

HE CAN'T HAVE COME TO ANY HARM. HE WAS HERE JUST NOW!

ANYWAY, I'VE GOT CLOVOGARLIX.

THAT'S SOMETHING...

LET'S GET BACK TO LUTETIA QUICKLY AND TRY TO FIND NAVISHTRIX! HE CAN LEAD US TO THE TRAFFICKERS' BOSS.

A LITTLE LATER...

WHO'LL BUY MY LETTUCE? LOVELY LUTETIA LETTUCE!

OLIVE OIL FROM GREECE!

SAVOURY LUGDUNUM SAUSAGE!

YOU KNOW, ASTERIX, I THINK IT'S MARKET DAY TODAY...

...AND A LITTLE FARTHER ON...

I WANT A STEAK, PLEASE.

A NICE PRIME STEAK?

THIS IS VERY GOOD MEAT...

AH! THAT'S BETTER!

OBELIX, LOOK!!! THERE HE IS!...

!!!

THAT'LL BE TWO SESTERTII...

WHAT THE...? IT'S NOT AS DEAR AS ALL THAT!

THERE HE IS! RUNNING THAT WAY!

STOP THIEF! MY STEAK! MY PRIME STEAK!!!

POC!

POC!

WHICH WAY DID HE GO?

WHAT'S ALL THAT COMMOTION?

MY PRIME STEAK!

33

BY APOLLO! YOU AGAIN!

I COULD SAY THE SAME THING, ROMAN!

?

GRAB HOLD OF THESE TWO MEN!!!

LOOK HERE, BE REASONABLE...

SHALL WE GET THEM, ASTERIX?

NO, OBELIX. I'M SURE WE SHALL BE ABLE TO EXPLAIN EVERYTHING.

WHAT ABOUT MY PRIME STEAK? WHO'S GOING TO PAY FOR MY PRIME STEAK?

SOON AFTERWARDS...

AVE, CENTURION! I'VE BROUGHT IN TWO GAULS!

WHAT ABOUT MY PRIME...

BY ALL THE GODS, THOSE TWO AGAIN!

LISTEN, ROMAN, WE CAN EXPLAIN EVERYTHING...

... STEAK!

NOT A WORD! PUT THEM IN CHAINS AND LOCK THEM UP SEPARATELY!

AND JUST WHAT ARE YOU GOING TO DO ABOUT MY PRIME STEAK?

I'LL SHOW YOU WHAT I'M GOING TO DO ABOUT YOUR PRIME STEAK!!

LATER...

DID YOU CATCH THE THIEF?

NO! GIVE ME A NICE STEAK!

ASTERIX AND THE CAULDRON

TEXT BY GOSCINNY

DRAWINGS BY UDERZO

TRANSLATED BY ANTHEA BELL AND DEREK HOCKRIDGE

GAULISH VILLAGE

COMPENDIUM

LAUDANUM

AQUARIUM

TOTORUM

ARMORICA

BELGICA

LUTETIA

GAUL
(ROMAN CONQUEST)
50 B.C.

CELTICA

PROVINCIA

AQUITANIA

e year is 50 BC. Gaul is entirely occupied by the Romans.
ell, not entirely... One small village of indomitable Gauls still
lds out against the invaders. And life is not easy for the
man legionaries who garrison the fortified camps of
torum, Aquarium, Laudanum and Compendium...

a few of the Gauls

Asterix, the hero of these adventures. A shrewd, cunning little warrior; all perilous missions are immediately entrusted to him. Asterix gets his superhuman strength from the magic potion brewed by the druid Getafix...

Obelix, Asterix's inseparable friend. A menhir delivery-man by trade; addicted to wild boar. Obelix is always ready to drop everything and go off on a new adventure with Asterix — so long as there's wild boar to eat, and plenty of fighting.

Getafix, the venerable village druid. Gathers mistletoe and brews magic potions. His speciality is the potion which gives the drinker superhuman strength. But Getafix also has other recipes up his sleeve...

Cacofonix, the bard. Opinion is divided as to his musical gifts. Cacofonix thinks he's a genius. Everyone else thinks he's un-speakable. But so long as he doesn't speak, let alone sing, everybody likes him...

Finally, Vitalstatistix, the chief of the tribe. Majestic, brave and hot-tempered, the old warrior is respected by his men and feared by his enemies. Vitalstatistix himself has only one fear; he is afraid the sky may fall on his head tomorrow. But as he always says, 'Tomorrow never comes.'

5

HAVE YOU COME ALL BY YOURSELF LIKE THAT?

OH, NO! HERE'S MY RETINUE.

?

WHAT THE.... IT'S A CAULDRON!

YES, THAT'S WHY I HAD TO WALK. THERE'S NOT MUCH ROOM ON THESE SHIELDS.

YOU MEAN YOU GAVE UP YOUR SHIELD TO THIS CAULDRON? WHAT'S SO SPECIAL ABOUT IT?

IT'S FULL OF SESTERTII, BY TOUTATIS! COME OVER HERE... I'VE GOT SOMETHING TO TELL YOU.

JULIUS CAESAR IS IN GRAVE FINANCIAL DIFFICULTIES. HE'S USED THE TAXES WHICH WERE GOING TO PAY HIS GARRISONS HERE IN GAUL TO EQUIP HIS ARMIES FOR NEW CAMPAIGNS...

I HEARD THAT CAESAR WAS ABOUT TO LEVY NEW TAXES, SO I PUT ALL MY PEOPLE'S SAVINGS IN THIS CAULDRON, AND I'VE BROUGHT IT TO YOU FOR SAFE KEEPING... I BELIEVE YOU DON'T PAY ANY TAXES?...

WELL, A TAX COLLECTOR DID SHOW UP ONE DAY.... WE HAVEN'T PAID ANY TAXES SINCE!

DEAR ME!... I'LL NEVER FORGET HOW WE SHOWED HIM UP!

WHAT FUN I'VE HAD! REMEMBER WHEN...?

OH, DO STOP! HOHOHO!

YOU MEAN HE NEVER RETURNED?

THAT'S RIGHT. NO RETURN, NO TAX RETURN, NO TAXES!

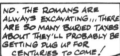

WE HAVE A DEBT OF HONOUR TO PAY, ASTERIX. CHIEF WHOSEMORALSARELASTIX ENTRUSTED A CAULDRON AND HIS SESTERTII TO US...

GIVE HIM BACK HIS CAULDRON! THAT WILL PAY OFF HALF THE DEBT, AND ...

SILENCE, OR I'LL HAVE THE VILLAGE CLEARED!!!

BANG! BANG! BANG!

IT WAS UP TO YOU TO LOOK AFTER THE CAULDRON, AND YOU FAILED IN YOUR DUTY. YOU HAVE BROUGHT DISHONOUR ON OUR VILLAGE. YOU KNOW HOW STRICT OUR LAWS ARE ...

SAD AS IT IS FOR US TO TAKE THIS STEP, YOU ARE BANISHED FROM THE VILLAGE. YOU MAY RETURN ONLY IF YOU MAKE UP FOR WHAT YOU HAVE DONE.

I SHALL RETURN WITH THE CAULDRON FULL OF SESTERTII, OR I SHALL NOT RETURN AT ALL!

WELL SPOKEN, BY TOUTATIS! COME BACK WITH YOUR CAULDRON OR IN YOUR CAULDRON!

YOU KNOW THE MAGIC POWERS OF THIS POTION. IT WILL GIVE YOU INVINCIBLE STRENGTH. NOW GO, MY BOY, AND USE IT WISELY!

THANKS, O DRUID!

PARP

ASTERIX IS LEAVING! WHERE'S HE GOING?!!

LET HIM BE, OBELIX, HE IS BANISHED, BUT PERHAPS HE WILL COME BACK SOME DAY.

ARE YOU ALL OFF YOUR HEADS? LETTING ASTERIX GO OFF LIKE THAT, ALL ALONE? HOW DO YOU EXPECT HIM TO GET BY IF DOGMATIX AND I AREN'T THERE TO ADVISE HIM?

TAP! TAP! TAP!

SOON AFTERWARDS...

CHIEF WHOSEMORALSARELASTIX MENTIONED SOME ROMANS ... PERHAPS THEY STOLE THE MONEY.

WE'RE NOT FAR FROM COMPENDIUM. LET'S GO AND ASK THEM ...

THE ENTRANCE TO THE FORTIFIED ROMAN CAMP OF COMPENDIUM ...

HALT! QUO VADIS? NO ENT...

SCHKONNK!

WHERE'S THE INFORMATION BUREAU?

THAT MUST BE THEIR CENTURION'S TENT OVER THERE.

GAULS? WHO GAVE YOU PERMISSION TO ENTER OUR CAMP?

THE CAULDRON.

WHAT CAULDRON?

THIS CAULDRON! WE'VE COME TO FILL IT!

FILL IT? WHAT WITH?

I'M NOT TOO CLEAR MYSELF, BUT ASTERIX CAN EXPLAIN IT ALL.

TO FILL IT WITH MONEY. OUR MONEY! MONEY! DO YOU GET IT? THE MONEY! THE MONEY!

THE MONEY?

THE MONEY!

OUR PAY HAS ARRIVED!

AND NOT A MOMENT TOO SOON! OUR MONEY! OUR MONEY!

NO LUCK! WE DIDN'T EVEN GET A MEAL!

I NEVER DID FIND THAT BOAR, THE ONE THAT WAS GOING TO HAVE CHESTNUT STUFFING

OH, NUTS! IT ISN'T EVEN THE CHESTNUT SEASON...

?. !!?

I'VE BEEN ROBBED! I'M GOING BACK! OH, WHAT A BORE!

COME ON! YOU AND YOUR HOARY OLD CHESTNUTS...

WHICH MAY EVEN HAVE BEEN HORSE CHESTNUTS, SINCE THE PIRATES HAVE CONKED OUT...

TALK ABOUT HORSE-PLAY! THEY CAME, THEY SAW, THEY CONKERED...

GALLEY

LIFE ASHORE ISN'T ALL PLAIN SAILING... COME ON, LADS, LET'S GET BACK TO SEA!

I DON'T THINK WE'RE GOING TO FIND THE THIEVES. WE MUST THINK OF SOMETHING ELSE...

WE'LL HAVE TO EARN THE MONEY.

EARN MONEY? BUT WE'VE NEVER DONE A THING LIKE THAT!

WELL, WE MUST START... BUT HOW?

SUPPOSE WE TOLD PEOPLE THE STORY OF OUR ADVENTURES? THEY MIGHT PAY TO LISTEN!

I'M NOT MUCH OF A BUSINESSMAN, BUT I CAN TELL YOU THAT WOULDN'T MAKE ANY MONEY!

WE COULD CALL THEM "THE ADVENTURES OF OBELIX THE GAUL" AND...

OH, SHUT UP!

LET'S SEE, WHAT CAN WE DO?

I CAN DELIVER MENHIRS, TRAIN DOGS, HUNT BOAR, FISH, EAT, DRINK, DANCE, BASH THE ROMANS...

LOOK! ON THE ROAD!

WHO ARE YOU?

WE'RE MERCHANTS, WE'RE GOING TO SELL OUR PRODUCE AT THE MARKET IN CONDATUM.

AND YOU EARN MONEY THERE?

I WOULDN'T SAY THAT. WHAT WITH THE ECONOMIC CRISIS AND TODAY'S PRICES... WE JUST ABOUT MAKE ENDS MEET.

I MUST BE OFF IF I'M TO GET A GOOD PITCH. FORWARD MARCH, YOU LOT! I CAN SEE ONE WHO ISN'T IN GOOSE-STEP!

THAT'S THE WAY TO FILL THE CAULDRON! WE'LL SELL THINGS AT THE MARKET!

SELL WHAT THINGS?

BOARS! WE CAN HUNT BOARS AND THEN SELL THEM!

THAT REMINDS ME, WE HAVEN'T EATEN YET!

BOARS, BOARS, BEST PR...

HOW MUCH ARE YOUR BOARS?

?

HOW MUCH?...ER... I DON'T KNOW... HOW MUCH WILL YOU GIVE ME?

HM...LET'S SEE THE GOODS...

THEY'RE NOT VERY BIG.

THERE, WHAT DID I TELL YOU? THEY'RE VERY SMALL!

SHUT UP, OBELIX!

NO, LET YOUR FRIEND HAVE HIS SAY! HE'S RIGHT! THEY'RE POOR QUALITY. NOW MINE...

THAT'S RIGHT, GO AND LOOK AT HIS... BOARS, BOARS, BEST PRIME BOARS!

HM... I'LL GIVE YOU FIVE SESTERTII.

FIVE SESTERTII FOR EACH BOAR?

ER... NO, FOR A DOZEN... I MEAN FOURTEEN. YOU'VE GOT JUST ENOUGH.

VERY WELL. DONE!

YOU'RE SELLING HIM FOURTEEN BOARS FOR FIVE SESTERTII?

YOU MIND YOUR OWN BUSINESS!

I'LL TAKE THEM AS THEY ARE; YOU NEEDN'T WRAP THEM UP.

HE'S TAKING THEM ALL!

FOR FIVE SESTERTII!

ASTERIX, I DON'T REALLY UNDERSTAND BUSINESS. WE HAD FOURTEEN BOARS, WE SOLD THEM, AND...

I KNOW, I KNOW...

I DON'T THINK WE'RE CUT OUT TO BE BUSINESSMEN... THE CAULDRON IS STILL AS EMPTY AS EVER, AND THE MAGIC POTION WON'T HELP US TO...

ENCORE! ENCORE!

BY THE RIGHT... QUICK MARCH!

CLAP! CLAP! CLAP! CLAP! CLAP! CLAP! CLAP!

ASTERIX, I'VE GOT IT! I'LL TELL YOU WHO'S GOING TO FILL OUR CAULDRON! DOGMATIX!

?!

I'LL TEACH HIM SOME TRICKS, AND PEOPLE WILL THROW US LOTS OF MONEY!

SIGH!

COME ALONG, DOGMATIX! BEG! LIKE THIS!

NOW, ON YOUR FRONT PAWS, LIKE THIS!

ROLL ALONG THE GROUND LIKE TH....

?

WOOF! WOOF! WOOF! WOOF! WOOFWOOF!

HARF! HARF! HARF!

WHO'S FIRST?

LUCKY BLIGHTER! HE'S SURE TO GET THE PRIZE!

NEXT!

PAFF!

AND NEXT COMES THE NEXT.

CHLAC!

AND THE NEXT!

... AND RUNNING PRACTICALLY NECK AND NECK, THE NEXT...

AND THE NEXT!

AND THE NEXT!

AND THE NEXT!

TCHON TCHOC! PAF!

... UNTIL AT LAST...

RIGHT, I THINK THAT'S THE LOT. NOW YOU CAN PAY ME.

TCHAC!

WHAT DO YOU MEAN, PAY YOU? YOUR FAT FRIEND DID IN ALL MY GLADIATORS, YOU'VE DONE IN MY ENTIRE AUDIENCE, YOU'VE GONE AND RUINED ME AND YOU WANT TO GET PAID AS WELL?

TAP! TAP! TAP! TAP!

YOU JUST GIVE ME BACK MY MAGNIFICENT WORKS OF ART!

WHAT FAT FRIEND?

O, GIVE HIM HIS STATUETTES, OBELIX.

27

THIS IS OUR THEATRE. LET ME INTRODUCE MYSELF: MY NAME IS LAURENSOLIVIUS.

MY AIM IS TO TRANSFORM THE MODERN DRAMA! WE HAVE A MESSAGE! A MISSION! WE MUST SHOCK OUR AUDIENCES! JERK THEM OUT OF THEIR LETHARGY! IT MUST ALL BE NATURAL AND SPONTANEOUS!

NOW, LET'S GET ON WITH THE REHEARSAL! TAKE UP YOUR POSITIONS!

?!?!?

ORGIES! ORGIES! WE WANT ORGIES!

HOLD ON A MOMENT! WHERE'S OUR DISGUSTED AUDIENCE? WHERE'S ALECGUINUS GOT TO ...? YOU'RE LATE, DUCKY.

JUST COMING!

RIGHT. START AGAIN.

ORGIES! WE WANT ...

YOU FORGOT ONE "ORGIES," DUCKY!

SORRY! ORGIES! ORGIES! WE WANT ORGIES!

STOP! THIS IS DISGRACEFUL! THEY'RE MAKING FUN OF US!

VERY GOOD, ALECGUINUS, VERY GOOD ... IT MIGHT BE AN IDEA IF YOU THREW THINGS AT HIM ...

NO, IT MIGHT NOT! THAT WOULD LOOK VULGAR!

29

ALL RIGHT. NOW, YOU TWO WAIT UPSTAGE, KEEPING QUITE STILL....

... AND THEN I SHALL POINT AT YOU - YES, YOU, FATSO....

HIS NAME IS OBELIX.

WHOSE NAME IS OBELIX?

... AND WHEN I GIVE THE SIGN, YOU COME UP TO THE FRONT OF THE STAGE, DOING A LITTLE DANCE, AND SAY SOMETHING: ANYTHING!

ANYTHING?

YES. THAT WILL BE THE END OF THE PLAY - A SPONTANEOUS CRY FROM THE HEART! JUST SAY WHATEVER COMES INTO YOUR HEAD!

BUT SOMETIMES NOTHING COMES INTO IT!

RIGHT! SEE YOU ALL THIS EVENING! WE MUST MAKE OUR MARK! WE HAVE TO GIVE THE PUBLIC WHAT IT WANTS: A MESSAGE!

BUT WHAT AM I GOING TO SAY? WHATEVER AM I GOING TO SAY?

OH, WHAT DOES IT MATTER? OUR CAULDRON IS THE IMPORTANT THING.

SO HOW ABOUT THE MESSAGE? DON'T YOU CARE ABOUT THE MESSAGE?

AND THAT EVENING, THE THEATRE FILLS UP WITH THE USUAL SCINTILLATING FIRST-NIGHT AUDIENCE: THE ROMAN PREFECT, THE OFFICERS OF THE GARRISON, ALL THE LOCAL BIGWIGS, IN FACT, EVERYONE WHO IS ANYONE IN CONDATUM.

I THINK THIS SHOULD BE ENTERTAINING, O PREFECT!

I HEAR THEY'RE QUITE DISGUSTING!

UNSPEAKABLE! I HAD A LOT OF TROUBLE GETTING SEATS!

THE SHOW STARTS...!

DING! DONG!

WHAT AN UGLY LOT YOU ARE! WE MAY BE UGLY TOO, BUT YOU'RE WORSE!

YAAAH!

IT'S SO DREADFULLY AUTHENTIC...!

ORGIES! ORGIES! WE WANT ORGIES!

STOP! STOP! THIS IS DISGRACEFUL! THEY'RE MAKING FUN OF US!

HE'S RIGHT!

NO, HE ISN'T!

THROW HIM OUT!

MUSEUM PIECES!

ROMAN RELICS!

THAT'S YOUR CUE! GO ON! GO ON, THEN!

I.... I'LL NEVER MAKE IT!

THINK OF THE CAULDRON!

SAY SOMETHING! COME ON ANYTHING! WHATEVER COMES INTO YOUR HEAD!

THESE ROMANS ARE CRAZY!

WHAT?

THAT'S GOING TOO FAR! ARREST THESE MORONS WHO DARE TO INSULT THE AUTHORITY OF ROME!

VERY WELL PRODUCED, THIS SHOW!

YES, IT'S GETTING GOOD!

THEY'RE OVERDOING IT A BIT NOW; THAT'S NOT VERY LIFELIKE.

OH, IT'S THE NEW DRAMATIC CONVENTION. PERSONALLY, I THINK IT'S EFFECTIVE.

COME ON! WE DON'T WANT TO HANG AROUND! THIS IS NONE OF OUR BUSINESS, WE'VE GOT BETTER THINGS TO DO.

LATER, OUTSIDE THE TOWN JAIL....

WOULD YOU LIKE US TO GET YOU OUT OF THERE?

NO FEAR! I'VE JUST BEEN BOOKED FOR THE CIRCUS AT ROME. A ONE-NIGHT STAND, OF COURSE, BUT WHAT A SHOW! LIONS, TIGERS, THE WHOLE WORKS! DEAD GOOD!

BY THE WAY, FATSO— YOU OUGHT TO GO IN FOR THE THEATRE, DEAR! WHAT PERSONALITY! WHAT A GALL!

Any idea just how we place a bet, Obelix?

Maybe I could help you, friends!

Let me introduce myself: Confidentius, I'm an expert. I can give you some tips.

You think we could fill our cauldron with your tips?

Sure! It's like this: the races are for chariots called quadrigae, each drawn by four horses... you can back them each way...

... that is, for a place in the first three, at reducing odds, which comes to twelve horses in all ...

?

But your best bet is to back the winner at full odds: the colours are blue, white, red and green... here come closer...

?

Put your money on the blues for the next race! I know a cousin by marriage of the Auriga*. He just can't lose!

* CHARIOTEER

30ᴬ

Give me your money, and I'll place your bet... all I ask is half your winnings.

You're sure he can't lose?

It's impossible... now, you go into the hippodrome, we'll meet at the exit.

30ᴮ

34

HARD LUCK, FRIENDS! BUT MY BROTHER-IN-LAW HAPPENS TO KNOW THE NEPHEW OF THE AURIGA OF THE GREEN CHARIOT IN THE NEXT RACE, AND HE...!!

WE HAVEN'T GOT ANY MORE MONEY! AND YOU TOLD ME IT WAS IMPOSSIBLE FOR THE BLUE CHARIOT TO LOSE!

IMPOSSIBLE IS NOT A GAULISH WORD, MY FRIENDS!

!

SIGH
SIGH
SIGH

SIGH

COME ON, OBELIX. I'VE STILL GOT A FEW BRONZE COINS LEFT. LET'S HAVE A BITE TO EAT.

SOON AFTERWARDS...

I RECOMMEND THE BOAR; IT'S VERY GOOD VALUE JUST NOW. PRICES HAVE FALLEN; BOAR ARE BEING SOLD FIFTEEN TO THE DOZEN AT THE MOMENT.

BARCLUS BANK

?

WHAT'S THAT? A TEMPLE?

NEAR ENOUGH. IT'S A ROMAN BANK. WHERE THEY KEEP THEIR GOLD.

YOU KNOW WHAT WE'RE GOING TO DO?

EAT OUR BOARS?

NO! WE ARE GOING TO ROB THAT BANK! THE ROMANS TAKE OUR MONEY, SO IT'S NO CRIME TO TAKE IT BACK FROM THEM!

BUT HOW DO YOU ROB A BANK?

I HAVE A PLAN... LANDLORD!

CLACK

CAN YOU LET US HAVE A ROOM WITH A VIEW OF THE BANK?

A VIEW OF THE BANK?

SC... SCRUNCH! SCRUNCH!

WELL, HAVE YOU GOT A ROOM WITH A VIEW OF THE SEA?

WHAT, IN CONDATUM? OF COURSE NOT!

RIGHT, ONE WITH A VIEW OF THE BANK, THEN!

THAT SEEM'S LOGICAL... FOLLOW ME.

SOON AFTERWARDS...

FINE. I'M OFF TO DO A BIT OF SHOPPING. MEANWHILE, I WANT YOU TO LOITER AROUND THE BANK, LOOKING INNOCENT. YOU MUST TRY AND FIND OUT WHAT TIME THE GUARD CHANGES, AND WHERE THEY KEEP THE GOLD.

SCRUNCH! SCRUNCH!

SCRUNCH! SCRUNCH!

LOOK INNOCENT? HOW DO I DO THAT?

HOW SHOULD I KNOW? YOU'RE SUPPOSED TO HAVE ALL THIS TALENT FOR ACTING... YOU CAN STROLL BY, WHISTLING NONCHALANTLY!

TRUE... I FORGOT MY TALENT FOR ACTING ... LET'S GO!

WE'LL MEET BACK AT THE INN. BE CAREFUL.

HEY! YOU THERE!

ME?

YES, YOU! YOU LOOK TO ME LIKE SOMEONE WHO'S THINKING OF ROBBING A BANK, BUT YOU HAVEN'T GOT A HOPE!

THE BANK IS CONSTANTLY GUARDED. THE GUARD CHANGES AT NOON, AT SIX IN THE EVENING AND AT MIDNIGHT, AND THERE ARE MEN INSIDE ALL NIGHT...

THE GOLD IS KEPT IN A CELLAR WITH A HEAVY IRON DOOR WHICH HAS A SECRET CATCH HIDDEN IN THE ORNAMENTAL MOULDING...

TAP! TAP! TAP!

..SO DON'T GO GETTING ANY IDEAS!

SOON AFTERWARDS...

I DIDN'T LEARN ANYTHING. HE SAW THROUGH ME BEFORE I COULD GET ANY IDEAS.

NEVER MIND, WE CAN WATCH THE SENTRIES COMING AND GOING FROM THIS WINDOW.

WE SHALL HAVE TO TAKE TURNS KEEPING WATCH... WRITE EVERYTHING DOWN, INCLUDING THE TIMES...

AND FOR TWO DAYS AND TWO NIGHTS...

... OUR FRIENDS TAKE TURNS.

THERE WE ARE, OBELIX! I'VE WORKED OUT THE TIMES THEY CHANGE GUARD!

I NOTICE THAT ABOUT ELEVEN IN THE MORNING THE SENTRY LEAVES HIS POST TO HAVE A DRINK OF WATER AT THE FOUNTAIN ...

ZZZ.. ZZZ

THAT'S OUR MOMENT TO ACT.

YAAAAWN!

LOOK, I'VE DRAWN UP A PLAN.

SCRATCH! SCRATCH!

SCRATCH SCRATCH!

BANK

ME

ROUTE TAKEN BY OBELIX

DOGMATIX

INN

35A

DOGMATIX WILL KEEP WATCH AND WARN US IF THE SENTRY COMES BACK SOONER THAN EXPECTED ... YOU BREAK DOWN THE DOOR ...

I'M HIDING BEHIND THE THIRD COLUMN. I LEAP IN ...

WE SHALL HAVE FIVE MINUTES TO CARRY OUT THE OPERATION BEFORE THE SENTRY GETS BACK. DURING THIS TIME, WE HAVE TO QUESTION THE STAFF AND FIND THE GOLD ... GET IT?

NO.

RIGHT. NEVER MIND. WE PLOUGH INTO THEM, WE PICK UP THE CASH, AND WE BEAT IT.

I GET THAT!

TOIIIING!

GLUG! GLUG! GLUG! GLUG!

35B

THIS DOOR WILL NEVER STAND UP TO THE MAGIC POTION!!!

BANG!

OH!

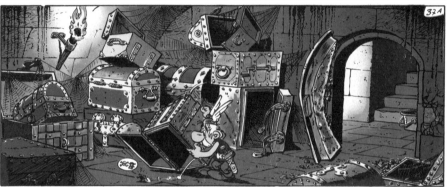

HEY, WHAT ARE YOU DOING HERE? IF YOU WANT TO DEPOSIT MONEY, YOU HAVE TO DO IT AT THE COUNTER UPSTAIRS.

I DIDN'T COME TO DEPOSIT MONEY, I CAME TO TAKE SOME.

OH, I THOUGHT IT WAS A BIT STRANGE!

BANG!

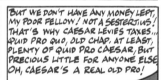

BUT WE DON'T HAVE ANY MONEY LEFT, MY POOR FELLOW! NOT A SESTERTIUS! THAT'S WHY CAESAR LEVIES TAXES... QUID PRO QUO, OLD CHAP, AT LEAST, PLENTY OF QUID PRO CAESAR, BUT PRECIOUS LITTLE FOR ANYONE ELSE! OH, CAESAR'S A REAL OLD PRO!

COME ALONG, OBELIX!

AND STOP THAT WHISTLING!

O.K.

41

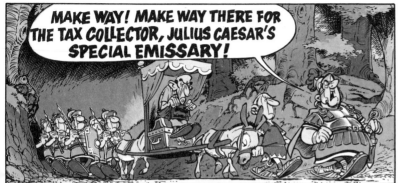

WHERE DOES CHIEF WHOSEMORALSARELASTIX LIVE?

UP THERE, RIGHT ON THE EDGE OF THE CLIFF.

O CHIEF WHOSEMORALSARELASTIX! HERE'S THE MONEY!

MONEY? WHERE? WHERE?

OH... IT'S YOU!

I AM RETURNING THE SESTERTII YOU ENTRUSTED TO MY CARE... I RATHER THINK THE TAX COLLECTOR HAS ALREADY CALLED?

THAT'S RIGHT... HE DIDN'T FIND ANY MONEY HERE, SO HE LEFT... WELL, THANKS VERY MUCH...

JUST A MOMENT!

?!

HOWEVER, THE CHIEF IS WRONG! HIS SESTERTII ARE NOT LOST TO THE ENTIRE HUMAN RACE... AT THE VERY MOMENT WHEN THE CAULDRON FALLS, A PIRATE SHIP IS SAILING PAST THE CLIFF...

CHLONK!

MUTINY! SUFFERING SEASERPENTS, WHO DARED CROWN ME WITH A CAULDRON!

AND FOR ONCE, JUST FOR ONCE, THE PIRATES ARE HAPPY!

ONION-FLAVOURED, TOO! MY FAVOURITE KIND!

SESTERTII FROM OLYMPUS! THIS SHOULD KEEP OUR HEADS ABOVE WATER!

AS HAPPY AS OUR FRIENDS, THE TOAST OF THE WHOLE VILLAGE, WHICH, THANKS TO THEM, HAS PRESERVED ITS HONOUR INTACT!

BUT WHAT I NEVER DID UNDERSTAND IS WHY ANYONE WOULD PUT MONEY IN THAT CAULDRON INSTEAD OF ONION SOUP IN THE FIRST PLACE!

THE END

UDERZO & GOSCINNY

ASTERIX AND THE NORMANS

TEXT BY GOSCINNY

DRAWINGS BY UDERZO

TRANSLATED BY ANTHEA BELL AND DEREK HOCKRIDGE

GAULISH VILLAGE

COMPENDIUM

LAUDANUM

AQUARIUM

TOTORUM

ARMORICA

BELGICA

LUTETIA

SPQR

GAUL

(ROMAN CONQUEST)

50 B.C.

CELTICA

PROVINCIA

AQUITANIA

e year is 50 BC. Gaul is entirely occupied by the Romans.
ll, not entirely... One small village of indomitable Gauls still
ds out against the invaders. And life is not easy for the
man legionaries who garrison the fortified camps of
orum, Aquarium, Laudanum and Compendium...

a few of the Gauls

Asterix, the hero of these adventures. A shrewd, cunning little warrior; all perilous missions are immediately entrusted to him. Asterix gets his superhuman strength from the magic potion brewed by the druid Getafix...

Obelix, Asterix's inseparable friend. A menhir delivery-man by trade; addicted to wild boar. Obelix is always ready to drop everything and go off on a new adventure with Asterix — so long as there's wild boar to eat, and plenty of fighting.

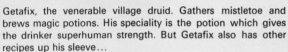

Getafix, the venerable village druid. Gathers mistletoe and brews magic potions. His speciality is the potion which gives the drinker superhuman strength. But Getafix also has other recipes up his sleeve...

Cacofonix, the bard. Opinion is divided as to his musical gifts. Cacofonix thinks he's a genius. Everyone else thinks he's unspeakable. But so long as he doesn't speak, let alone sing, everybody likes him...

Finally, Vitalstatistix, the chief of the tribe. Majestic, brave and hot-tempered the old warrior is respected by his men and feared by his enemies. Vitalstatistix himself has only one fear; he is afraid the sky may fall on his head tomorrow. But as he always says, 'Tomorrow never comes.'

WATCH OUT!

BY TOUTATIS!

HE'S CRAZY!

CLUCK CLUCK

YELP YELP YELP

I SHALL THROW THE ARMS AND ARMOUR FIRM'S MAIL ORDER CATALOGUE AT HIM IF HE DOESN'T LOOK OUT!

SCREEEECH!!

YELP YELP YELP

HI, UNCLE! I'M YOUR NEPHEW JUSTFORKIX!

?!

ER... VERY NICE TO SEE YOU, JUSTFORKIX... LET ME INTRODUCE ASTERIX AND OBELIX...

I'VE NEVER SEEN A CHARIOT LIKE THAT BEFORE...

NO, YOU WOULDN'T GET MANY OF THESE AROUND HERE... IT'S A SPORTS CHARIOT MADE IN MEDIOLANUM*...

*MILAN

RIGHT, LET'S START.

START WHAT?

START MAKING A MAN OF HIM, OF COURSE! THE WAY TO START MAKING A MAN OF HIM IS TO START THUMPING HIM!

NO, NO, THAT'S NOT THE WAY.

OH, AND JUST HOW DOES MISTER ASTERIX THINK WE'RE GOING TO START MAKING A MAN OF HIM IF WE DON'T START THUMPING HIM SO AS TO START MAKING A MAN OF HIM?

WE WANT HIM TO TRUST US!

WE'RE GOING TO HOLD A BALL IN YOUR HONOUR, JUSTFORKIX!

YOU PEASANTS DANCE OUT HERE IN THE STYX?*

?!?

* GLOOMY CLASSICAL ALLUSION

HOW QUAINT!

YOU KNOW, OBELIX, I'M NOT SURE YOU WEREN'T RIGHT ABOUT THUMPING HIM!

SEE?

WOOF!

6

WHILE ALL THIS IS GOING ON IN GAUL, LET US TRAVEL FAR AWAY, TO THE NORTHERN LANDS WHERE WINTERS ARE HARD AND THE NIGHT LASTS FOR MONTHS ON END... LANDS INHABITED BY *THE NORSEMEN,* OR NORMANS, AS THE PEOPLE OF GAUL KNEW THEM. THEY ARE GREAT CONQUERORS...

WE GIVE THE GAULS A MISS FOR ONCE AND THAT LOT MAKE A NORMAN CONQUEST OF US!

THEY WORSHIP THOR, THE GOD OF WAR, AND ODIN, WHO INVITES WARRIORS SLAIN IN BATTLE TO FEAST WITH HIM IN VALHALLA...

WON'T!

AND THEY DO NOT KNOW THE MEANING OF FEAR!

IF YOU DON'T FINISH YOUR NICE CREAM SOUP THE TROLL WILL COME AND EAT YOU UP!

BY THOR, THAT'S A LAUGH!

THIS IS A NUISANCE, SINCE NOT ONLY ARE THE CHILDREN NOT SCARED OF TROLLS, BUT AS FEAR OF THE AUTHORITIES ENCOURAGES PRUDENCE, NORSE ROADS ARE FAR FROM SAFE...

WHAT DO YOU MEAN BY IT, TRYING TO PASS A FOUR-REINDEER-POWER POLICE CHARIOT AT THE TOP OF A HILL???

SO WHAT? MINE'S A NORSE-DRAWN CHARIOT!

...AND IT IS PRACTICALLY IMPOSSIBLE TO CURE HICCUPS...

HAVE YOU OR HAVE YOU NOT FINISHED HICCUPPING?

HIC! NO. HIC! WHY DO YOU ASK?

HOPING TO LEARN THE MEANING OF FEAR, OLD NORSE SCHOLARS CARRY OUT SCIENTIFIC EXPERIMENTS...

FEEL ANYTHING?

NO FEAR SO FAR, ONLY PAIN. HAVE ANOTHER GO.

SO CHIEF OLAF TIMANDAHAF ASSEMBLES HIS MEN...

WE CAN'T GO ON LIKE THIS! EVEN THE WEAKEST OF NATIONS KNOW ABOUT FEAR AND BEING FRIGHTENED... BUT NOT US!

AND WE PRIDE OURSELVES ON KNOWING EVERYTHING! EVERY THING!

THUMP! THUMP! THUMP!

BUT LISTEN, O TIMANDAHAF, WHAT USE IS THIS THING FEAR THAT WE DON'T UNDERSTAND?

I'VE HEARD THAT FEAR LENDS YOU WINGS, BY ODIN. ONCE WE CAN FLY LIKE BIRDS WE'LL STICK AT NOTHING.

BY THOR!

BY ODIN!

BY GUM...

THE NOR... THE NOR... THE NORM...

SEE, THAT'S LUTETIANS FOR YOU! THEY'RE ALWAYS IN A HURRY IN LUTETIA... JUST CAN'T TAKE LIFE AS IT COMES!

LUTETIA'S ALL RIGHT FOR A VISIT, BUT I DON'T FANCY LIVING THERE.

OH, I WAS LOOKING FOR YOU. I'VE BEEN THINKING ABOUT THE HIT I MIGHT MAKE IN LUTE...

CLUCK!

CLU... EEEK!

WHAT'S THE MATTER WITH HIM?

IT SEEMS THE NORMANS WANT TO INVADE US.

WE'RE OFF TO SEE THE CHIEF ABOUT IT. JUSTFORKIX WILL BE THERE BY NOW.

GOOD. I WANT TO ASK HIM ABOUT THE PALACE OF VARIETIX.

SOON AFTERWARDS.

YOU TWO GO AND SEE WHAT THE NORMANS ARE DOING. IF THEY'RE LANDING, WE THROW THEM BACK INTO THE SEA.

DO YOU THINK THEY'LL LAND, ASTERIX? HEY, DO YOU REALLY THINK SO?

I'LL GO AND MAKE A LITTLE MAGIC POTION, JUST IN CASE...

PSST... I WANT A WORD WITH YOU...

WELL, NORMANS APART, DO YOU LIKE IT HERE? NOT FEELING HOMESICK?

LIS... LISTEN, DO YOU KNOW WHO THE NORMANS ARE?

OF COURSE! THEY'RE FIERCE FIGHTERS, AND LIKE US THEY DON'T KNOW THE MEANING OF FEAR!

WE MAY LIVE IN THE PROVINCES, MY BOY, BUT THAT DOESN'T MEAN WE'RE OUT OF TOUCH!

CRAZY! THEY'RE ALL CRAZY!

RIGHT, CAN WE HAVE A TALK ABOUT MY FUTURE NOW?

IN THE NORMAN CAMP, OLAF TIMANDAHAF IS JUST FINISHING A SOLE IN CREAM SAUCE...

NESCAF, I WANT YOU TO GO SCOUTING... SPY OUT THE LAND, SEE WHAT SORT OF PEOPLE THESE GAULS ARE!

RIGHT, O CHIEF TIMANDAHAF!

OUR VOYAGES ARE VERY EDUCATIONAL... WE LEARN ABOUT THE NATIVES BEFORE WE SLAUGHTER THEM.

I THINK I'LL HIDE IN THIS FOREST.

I'LL BE ALL RIGHT HERE... HULLO, THERE'S SOMEONE COMING...

WHAT DO YOU THINK THE NORMANS ARE GOING TO DO, ASTERIX?

WHO CARES? THEY WON'T SCARE US... WE DON'T KNOW THE MEANING OF FEAR! WE'VE NEVER BEEN FRIGHTENED OF ANYONE YET!

OH NO! WE'VE COME ALL THIS WAY FOR NOTHING...

HULLO, JUSTFORKIX? COMING TO HUNT BOAR WITH US?

HOW DO YOU LUTETIANS HUNT BOAR? HEREABOUTS WE JUST THUMP THEM AND THEN...

NO, I WANT TO ASK YOU A FAVOUR ... LOOK, THE CLIMATE HERE DOESN'T AGREE WITH ME TOO WELL. WILL YOU HELP ME PERSUADE MY UNCLE TO LET ME GO HOME TO LUTETIA...?

YOU'RE FRIGHTENED OF THE NORMANS, AREN'T YOU?

YEEEEES! I'M SO FRIGHTENED! I'M MORE FRIGHTENED THAN ANYONE ELSE IN THE WORLD! BOOHOOOOOOO!

YOU MUSTN'T BE FRIGHTENED, JUSTFORKIX... HAVE NO FEAR, WE'RE WITH YOU... NOW, YOU CAN'T BE FRIGHTENED WITH US HERE, CAN YOU?

SNIFF! NO, I DON'T FEEL SO FRIGHTENED NOW...

SPOILSPORT!

12

16

TIMANDAHAF IS JUST FINISHING HIS VEAL IN CREAM SAUCE...

OH, SO YOU'RE BACK, NESCAF. WHAT NEWS?

I'VE BEEN LISTENING TO SOME OF THE GAULS. THEY DON'T KNOW THE MEANING OF FEAR EITHER.

WHAT? YOU MEAN WE'VE COME ALL THIS WAY FOR NO GOOD REASON?

CRACK!

I'VE A GOOD MIND TO PUT US ALL TO THE SWORD... MAYBE WE'LL LEARN THE REASON* FOR FEAR AT ODIN'S FEAST* SINCE THESE GAULS ARE SO IGNORANT!

THEY DO AS GOOD A SOLE* AS WE COULD GET FROM OUR OWN ICE FLOES, THOUGH...

*SENTIMENTS ECHOED CENTURIES LATER BY ALEXANDER POPE... 'THE FEAST OF REASON AND THE FLOW OF SOUL...'

ANYWAY, DON'T BOOK OUR TABLE YET! I DID HEAR ONE GAUL BOAST HE WAS AN EXPERT ON FEAR...

A REAL PROFESSIONAL, BY THOR! THAT'S WHAT WE NEED!

THE ONLY THING IS, WHEN HE'S WITH THE OTHER GAULS HE ISN'T SO FRIGHTENED...

GET AN EXPEDITIONARY FORCE TOGETHER! WE MUST CAPTURE HIM AND SHIELD HIM FROM THE DEBILITATING INFLUENCE OF HIS FRIENDS!

FEAR WILL LEND US WINGS, AND WE'LL SOON BE AIRBORNE... HAVE A LITTLE SKULL, NESCAF?

I WON'T SAY NO... LET'S PUT OUR HEADS TOGETHER.

MEANWHILE, IN THE GAULISH VILLAGE...

I... I'VE DECIDED TO CUT MY HOLIDAY SHORT AND GO BACK TO LUTETIA...

WHAT, JUST WHEN THE REAL FUN'S STARTING? OH, DON'T GO, JUSTFORKIX! YOU'LL LEARN HOW TO FIGHT! WE GAULS NEVER GIVE QUARTER!

I PROMISE YOU THERE WON'T BE ANY GAULISH QUARTER!

I KNOW, BUT THERE'S A LATIN QUARTER AND I'D LIKE TO GET BACK TO IT!

13

IN THE NORMAN CAMP, WHERE TIMANDAHAF IS JUST FINISHING A CHICKEN IN CREAM SAUCE...

WE GOT HIM, O TIMANDAHAF!

BY ODIN! LET'S GO AND SEE HIM RIGHT AWAY, O NESCAF!

HE DOESN'T LOOK TOO GOOD, NESCAF!

WE CLUBBED HIM TO STOP HIM FLYING AWAY, THE WAY WE CLUB BIRDS... NOT VERY TOUGH, THIS GAULISH RIFFRAFF!

COMING!

NO, NO ONE WANTS YOU, RIFFRAF!

RIGHT. BRING HIM ROUND. COME HERE, ALL! MAKE HASTE!

SPLASH!

HASTING'S THE WORD... SURELY IT'S NOT 1066 YET?

WHO... WHAT...? HELP!

BY TOUTATIS, THIS IS THE END OF ME! ALL THESE NORMANS... SO MANY OF THEM! THEY LOOK SO FIERCE... HELP! THEY'RE GOING TO KILL ME... THEIR CHIEF IS COMING TOWARDS ME...

GO ON, THEN! FRIGHTEN US!

JUSTFORKIX, KIDNAPPED? WELL, HE MAY NOT BE A VERY DUTIFUL SON AND NEPHEW... BUT WHY WOULD THEY KIDNAP HIM?

PERHAPS THEY WANTED SOME DUTY-FREE GOODS TO TAKE HOME.

ASTERIX AND OBELIX, GO OFF TO THE NORMAN CAMP AND SEE IF JUSTFORKIX IS THERE!

I'VE MADE YOU A LITTLE MAGIC POTION JUST IN CASE, ASTERIX.

THANKS, O GETAFIX.

I...

NO! YOU KNOW YOU'VE BEEN STRONG ENOUGH TO UPROOT A TREE SINCE YOU FELL IN THE POTION AS A BABY!

NO, HONESTLY! THE EFFECTS HAVE WORN OFF... WATCH THIS...

TEEHEE! I'M GOING TO PRETEND I CAN'T UPROOT A TREE AND THEN HE'LL GIVE ME SOME POTION! CUNNING, EH? TEEHEE!

LOOK! ARE YOU ALL WATCHING?

WE'RE WATCHING!

!?!

CREEEAK!

I UPROOT IT EVEN WHEN I'M ONLY PRETENDING!

HAHAHAHA!

BOOHOOHOOO!

WHAT'S THE MATTER WITH HIM?

DOGMATIX DOESN'T LIKE PEOPLE HURTING TREES... HE LOVES TREES... I WON'T DO IT AGAIN, DOGMATIX, I PROMISE!

SNIFF!

19

23

* EAGER BEAVER. BUT DESPITE THE CASTOR ACTION FAVOURED BY OLEAGINUS, AMORICAN CAMPAIGNS SELDOM WENT ON OILED WHEELS.

SO WHAT KIND OF EXPERT IS YOUNG JUSTFORKIX?

AS IF YOU DIDN'T KNOW!

HE'S AN EXPERT ON FEAR, BY THOR! WE'RE COUNTING ON HIM TO TEACH US THE MEANING OF FEAR... WHETHER HE LIKES IT OR NOT!

???

AND IF HE WON'T WE'RE GOING TO THROW HIM OFF A CLIFFTOP TO WATCH HIM FLY!

ASTERIX, IF YOU ASK ME, THESE NORMANS ARE...

LET ME THINK A MOMENT, OBELIX.

IF WE TEACH YOU THE MEANING OF FEAR, WILL YOU GIVE US BACK OUR EXPERT AND GO AWAY?

YES. WE DIDN'T COME HERE TO MAKE WAR. WE'LL LEAVE THAT TO OUR DESCENDANTS A FEW CENTURIES FROM NOW...

WELL, WE'VE GOT SOMETHING IN OUR VILLAGE WHICH WILL DO THE TRICK. BUT WE'LL HAVE TO GO AND FETCH IT.

27A

ALL RIGHT, BUT ONE OF YOU STAYS HERE AS A HOSTAGE!

AND IF THE OTHER ONE DOESN'T COME BACK WE SHALL USE THE HOSTAGE'S SKULL FOR APPLE BRANDY!

PSSSPSSSPSSS!

BUT WHY MUST I GO? YOU'LL HAVE ALL THE FUN! YOU'LL GET BOAR IN CREAM SAUCE! IT'S THE THOUGHT OF THAT APPLE BRANDY GOING TO YOUR HEAD...

STOP ARGUING, OBELIX. THIS ISN'T THE RIGHT MOMENT.

NOT THE RIGHT MOMENT! NOT THE RIGHT MOMENT! IT NEVER IS THE RIGHT MOMENT FOR MISTER ASTERIX...

I'M LANDED WITH ALL THE HARD WORK...

BOMM!

27B

HOOOWWWL! HOOOWL!

EVERYONE TAKES ADVANTAGE OF MY WEAKNESS!

CRAAAAASH!

31

HI, OBELIX!

HUH!

SNIF!

HEY, POLYTECHNIX, WHERE'S CACOFONIX? HE ISN'T AT HOME.

I'M GLAD TO SAY I HAVEN'T THE SLIGHTEST IDEA!

YOU'D BETTER GO AND ASK THE CHIEF, OBELIX.

HE'S LOOKING FOR THE BARD!

I THOUGHT HE WAS ACTING STRANGELY!

... AND IF I CAN'T FIND CACOFONIX, WHAT ABOUT ASTERIX AND JUSTFORKIX? WE CAN'T GIVE THE NORMANS THEIR HEADS! WE MUST DO SOMETHING!

BY TOUTATIS, LET'S HAVE A LOOK AT THE BARD'S HUT!

SOON AFTERWARDS.

HE'S TAKEN ALL HIS MUSICAL INSTRUMENTS AND NEARLY ALL HIS CLOTHES... HE REALLY HAS LEFT!

I NEVER THOUGHT WE'D BE SORRY TO SEE THE BACK OF OUR BARD... BUT NOW HE'S THE KEY TO OUR TROUBLES, HE'S OFF!

OFF KEY, AS USUAL!

I'VE GOT AN IDEA!

YOU HAVE, OBELIX?

WHILE ASTERIX IS HELD HOSTAGE BY THE NORMANS...

OBELIX IS SURE TO COME BACK, TIMANDAHAF, NEVER FEAR!

WHAT DO YOU MEAN, NEVER FEAR??!!

...OBELIX GOES TIRELESSLY ON IN PURSUIT OF CACOFONIX THE BARD...

NEVER MIND, DOGMATIX! I'LL TEACH YOU TO SNIFF OUT BARDS AND YOU'LL GROW INTO A BIG STRONG DOGGIE...

...PICKING THE ODD BOAR ALONG HIS WAY TO STILL THE PANGS OF HUNGER...

...WHAT A COUPLE WE SHALL MAKE, WITH MY BRAINS AND YOUR STRENGTH!

...AND CASUALLY ELIMINATING SUCH ROMAN PATROLS AS ARE MISGUIDED ENOUGH TO CROSS HIS PATH.

NO POINT IN STOPPING HIM... SOL LUCET OMNIBUS, AS WE SAY AT HOME. LET'S GO BACK AND CARVE A REPORT IN TRIPLICATE.

GETTING TO BE A REAL CHISELLER, AREN'T YOU?

WHOA THERE! CALM DOWN! STOP REARING! WHOA!

?

WE MET A MAN MAKING SUCH AWFUL NOISES MY OXEN STAMPEDED!

YOU SEE, WE MUST BE ON THE RIGHT TRACK, DOGMATIX! THIS IS THE WAY TO FOLLOW A BARD'S SCENT!

OH YES, I SAW A HORSEMAN GO BY, BUT THE WAY HE WAS SINGING HE CAN'T HAVE BEEN A BARD!

MOOooo!

OH YES, HE CAME THIS WAY. THE MILK TURNED JUST THEN!

AND FURTHER ON...

CACOFONIX'S HORSE! WE'VE FOUND HIM! YOU SEE, DOGMATIX, THERE'S NO DIFFERENCE BETWEEN BARDS AND MENHIRS!

SELFSERVIX

THINGS ARE GOING FROM BAD TO WORSE IN THE NORMAN CAMP...

THESE SAUSAGES IN CREAM SAUCE ARE VERY GOOD!

SHUT UP, BY THOR!

BANG!

YOU'RE HAVING ME ON! I WON'T WAIT ANY LONGER! THE HOSTAGES WILL BE EXECUTED! SOMEONE GO AND GET THE GAULISH EXPERT OFF THE LONGSHIP!

LONGSHIP?

ONE OF OUR VESSELS. WE CAN USE EITHER SAIL OR OARS.

I KNEW YOUR FAVOURITE SPORT WAS SCULLING!

PUT THIS ONE IN CHAINS AND TAKE THEM BOTH UP THE CLIFF!

SOON AFTERWARDS...

I DON'T KNOW WHAT'S KEEPING OBELIX, BUT YOU MIGHT WAIT A LITTLE LONGER...

NO, I MIGHT NOT! YOU TWO HAVE A TABLE BOOKED FOR THE NEXT SITTING AT ODIN'S BANQUET!

BUT FIRST, IN THE CAUSE OF SCIENCE, YOU'RE GOING TO FLY OFF THIS CLIFF!

WOULDN'T YOU RATHER I GROVELLED AT YOUR FEET?

CHEER UP, JUSTFORKIX! SHOW THESE NORMANS HOW BRAVELY A GAUL CAN DIE!

YOU WAIT, THEY HAVEN'T FINISHED THEIR FUN YET!

RIGHT, I WANT YOU TO FLY OVER THERE TO THE LEFT. AFTER THAT I WANT YOU TO...

DON'T WORRY ABOUT THE ROUTE. IT'S NON-STOP, DIRECT...

37

39

41

AFTER THEIR FIRST FLIGHT, WHICH IS SHORT AND SHARP, THE NORMANS REJOIN THEIR SHIP...

...BUT ONCE THEY ARE BACK ON BOARD, THINGS SOMEHOW SEEM DIFFERENT...

GET UP INTO THE CROW'S NEST, TOOCLEVERBYHAF!

THE TROUBLE IS...

WELL?

I FEEL SO FRIGHTENED UP THERE ALL ON MY OWN.

GET UP THAT MAST!

YES, CHIEF!

CHIC!

EEEK!

CHIEF!

DON'T SNEAK UP BEHIND ME LIKE THAT! IT FRIGHTENS ME. WHAT DO YOU WANT?

IT'S THE MEN, CHIEF... THEY WANT YOU TO STOP SHOUTING LIKE THAT. IT FRIGHTENS THEM.

I FEAR OUR VOYAGE HAS BEEN ONLY TOO SUCCESSFUL...

SCRATCH! SCRATCH!

NEVER MIND, WE CAN FLY NOW...

FLY DOWN HERE, TOOCLEVERBYHAF!

YES, CHIEF!

SPLATCH!

YOU... YOU DON'T THINK THEY WERE HAVING US ON, CHIEF?

MAYBE, MAYBE NOT... ANYWAY, WE MUST BE CAREFUL IN FUTURE!

43

47

BACK IN THE VILLAGE OUR FRIENDS GET A TRIUMPHANT RECEPTION...

COME ON, THEN! WHY DON'T THEY COME ON?

SNIFF! SNIFF!

YES, O CHIEF VITALSTATISTIX, YOUR NEPHEW IS NOW A TRUE FEARLESS GAUL!

I KNEW I COULD COUNT ON YOU, ASTERIX!

OBELIX TAKES JUSTFORKIX IN HAND...

I'LL TEACH YOU HOW TO HUNT... WE'LL START WITH RABBITS, GO ON TO ROMAN PATROLS, AND WORK OUR WAY UP TO WILD BOAR!

LIKE MANY OTHER STARS, THE BARD LIKES TO DESCRIBE HIS HITS...

THEY STAMPED, THEY JUMPED UP AND DOWN, THEY TRIED TO GET AT ME!

YOU SHOULD GO FAR...THE FARTHER THE BETTER.

O GETAFIX, DO YOU THINK THE NORMANS HAD THE RIGHT IDEA WHEN THEY WANTED TO KNOW THE MEANING OF FEAR?

OF COURSE, ASTERIX!

IT'S ONLY WHEN YOU KNOW FEAR THAT YOU BECOME TRULY BRAVE! COURAGE LIES IN OVERCOMING YOUR FEAR!

AND SURE ENOUGH, THE NORMANS HAVE FOUGHT THEIR FEAR AND OVERCOME IT. THEY ARE STILL BRAVE, AND THEIR TABLES ARE BOOKED IN VALHALLA!

I ONLY ASKED IF THEY'D MADE ANY GOOD CONQUESTS LATELY.

YOU MIGHT HAVE KNOWN THAT WAS A NORSE CHESTNUT!

AS FOR JUSTFORKIX, HIS HOLIDAY IN THE BRACING AIR OF ARMORICA IS OVER. THE TIME HAS COME FOR HIM TO GO HOME TO LUTETIA. THE VILLAGERS GIVE HIM A SPLENDID FAREWELL BANQUET, AND CACOFONIX IS INVITED, SINCE IT IS, AFTER ALL, THANKS TO THE BARD THAT ALL'S WELL THAT ENDS WELL... OH YEAH!

UDERZO & GOSCINNY

THE END

ASTERIX AND THE GREAT CROSSING

TEXT BY GOSCINNY

DRAWINGS BY UDERZO

TRANSLATED BY ANTHEA BELL AND DEREK HOCKRIDGE

GAUL
(ROMAN CONQUEST)
50 B.C.

BELGICA

LUTETIA

ARMORICA

CELTICA

PROVINCIA

AQUITANIA

GAULISH VILLAGE

COMPENDIUM

LAUDANUM

AQUARIUM

TOTORUM

e year is 50 BC. Gaul is entirely occupied by the Romans.
l, not entirely… One small village of indomitable Gauls still
ds out against the invaders. And life is not easy for the
man legionaries who garrison the fortified camps of
orum, Aquarium, Laudanum and Compendium…

a few of the Gauls

Asterix, the hero of these adventures. A shrewd, cunning little warrior; all perilous missions are immediately entrusted to him. Asterix gets his superhuman strength from the magic potion brewed by the druid Getafix...

Obelix, Asterix's inseparable friend. A menhir delivery-man by trade; addicted to wild boar. Obelix is always ready to drop everything and go off on a new adventure with Asterix — so long as there's wild boar to eat, and plenty of fighting.

Getafix, the venerable village druid. Gathers mistletoe and brews magic potions. His speciality is the potion which gives the drinker superhuman strength. But Getafix also has other recipes up his sleeve...

Cacofonix, the bard. Opinion is divided as to his musical gifts. Cacofonix thinks he's a genius. Everyone else thinks he's unspeakable. But so long as he doesn't speak, let alone sing, everybody likes him...

Finally, Vitalstatistix, the chief of the tribe. Majestic, brave and hot-tempered, the old warrior is respected by his men and feared by his enemies. Vitalstatistix himself has only one fear; he is afraid the sky may fall on his head tomorrow. But as he always says, 'Tomorrow never comes.'

9

THROW OUT THE NET, OBELIX!

AYE, AYE, SIR!

HOW DO WE GET THE NET BACK NOW?

JUST PULL IT IN.

PULL IT IN? BUT I'VE THROWN IT OUT!

YOU MEAN TO SAY YOU DIDN'T TIE IT TO SOMETHING FIRST?

YOU MUST BE CRAZY, THROWING A NET OUT LIKE THAT!

YOU TOLD ME TO THROW IT OUT, SO I DID THROW IT OUT!

I'M A MENHIR DELIVERY-MAN, I AM! NOT A FISHERMAN!

ALL RIGHT, CALM DOWN. WE'LL JUST HAVE TO GO BACK FOR ANOTHER NET.

THE WIND'S TOO STRONG! WE CAN'T GO ABOUT!

HUH! HE LAUGHS AT ME AND HE CAN'T EVEN SAIL A BOAT!

I DON'T NEED ANY MENHIR DELIVERY-MEN GIVING ME ADVICE!

10

LET'S KEEP CALM, OBELIX. THIS BOAT SEEMS VERY SEAWORTHY; PERHAPS THE WIND WILL HAVE DIED DOWN TOMORROW. GOOD NIGHT.

GOOD NIGHT, ASTERIX! GOOD NIGHT, DOGMATIX!

WOOF!

ZZZZ

ZZZZ

ZZZ...SNIFF?

GRRRRRR!

ASTERIX! DOGMATIX HAS PICKED UP A SCENT!

TELL HIM TO GO TO SLEEP. THERE'S NOTHING AROUND HERE EXCEPT US.

GRRRØØÅÅRRR!

7A

DID YOU HEAR THAT, ASTERIX?

YES...

PERHAPS IT'S A MONSTER! WE'VE COME TO THE EDGE OF THE SEA, WHERE CREATURES FROM THE DEPTHS OF HELL...

TAKE IT EASY, OBELIX!!!

NEAR BY...

BY ÅLL THE GØDS! VØICES! WHÅT HÅVE YØU GØT US INTØ, HERENDETHELESSEN?

STEÅDY, STEPTØÅNSSEN! PERHÅPS IT'S THE SIRENS TRYING TØ LURE US WITH THEIR MELØDIØUS SØNG. LET'S STØP UP ØUR EÅRS!

WE'LL NEVER GET ØUT ØF THIS, HERENDETHELESSEN...? HERENDETHELESSEN? HERENDETHELESSEN!!!

WHÅT?

ØH! I THØUGHT YØU'D LEFT.

STØP UP YØUR EÅRS ÅND SHUT UP!!!

BUT EVEN THE DARKEST NIGHTS COME TO AN END, AND THE SUN RISES, FAR AWAY FROM THESE MYSTERIOUS INCIDENTS...

7B

YOU SEE? WE HAVEN'T COME TO THE EDGE OF THE SEA, THERE AREN'T ANY MONSTERS, AND THE WIND'S DIED DOWN.

WE CAN'T SEE LAND ANY MORE...

WE'LL TURN BACK HOME AS SOON AS WE GET A FAVOURABLE BREEZE. WE'VE JUST GOT TO WAIT.

I'M HUNGRY!

THINK OF SOMETHING ELSE.

IF YOU HADN'T TOLD ME TO THROW OUT THE NET, WE COULD HAVE CAUGHT SOME FISH... I'D RATHER EAT A BOAR, OF COURSE.

I SAID THINK OF SOMETHING ELSE... THINK OF YOUR MENHIRS.

WITH THAT SAUCE IMPEDIMENTA MAKES, I COULD EAT A MENHIR... REMEMBER THAT SAUCE?

MMM, YES!... VERY GOOD, SPECIALLY WHEN SHE PUTS IN THOSE LITTLE ONIONS AND BITS OF BACON...

ASTERIX! I'M HUNGRY!

I'M HUNGRY TOO! IT'S YOU MAKING ME HUNGRY, GOING ON ABOUT MENHIRS WITH ONIONS!

?

GRRRRR

LOOK!

A SHIP!

THERE'S A SIGHT FOR SORE EYES, MY BOY!

IT'S VERY NICE OF YOU TO THINK OF CELEBRATING MY BIRTHDAY!

DONEC ERIS FELIX, MULTOS NUMERABIS AMICOS.

WHY DON'T YOU STOP MAKING SILLY REMARKS AND COME ON DECK TO SUMMON THE CREW INSTEAD? THEN WE'LL START THE PARTY!

SAIL ON THE STARBOARD TACK!

OH, NEVER MIND WHAT TACK SHE'S ON! WE'RE OFF THE HARD TACK FOR ONCE. COME ON, TUCK IN, ME HEARTIES!

HELP! LOOK! THAT REALLY TAKES THE BISCUIT! IT'S THEM!

THEY'RE NOT BOTHERING TO STOP!

COME ON, WE'LL CATCH THEM UP. THERE'S NO WIND, SO YOU'LL HAVE TO PUSH.

13

WELL, WELL, WELL! IT'S OUR OLD FRIENDS!

SHALL WE GET THEM? SHALL WE GET THEM?

JUST A MOMENT. HOW ABOUT A CHANGE IN THE SCRIPT? IT'S MY BIRTHDAY TODAY... YOU WOULDN'T WANT TO SPOIL MY BIRTHDAY, WOULD YOU? JUST TELL ME WHAT YOU WANT AND THEN GO AWAY THIS ONCE WITHOUT SINKING ANYTHING.

OH, WE'RE ONLY LOOKING FOR A BITE TO EAT!

ASTERIX! LOOK WHAT I'VE FOUND!

WE DON'T WANT TO BE TOO GREEDY; WE'LL LEAVE YOU THIS SAUSAGE. HAPPY BIRTHDAY!

SOON AFTERWARDS...

HAPPY BIRTHDAY TO YOU, HAPPY BIRTHDAY TO YOU...

ALL RIGHT, DON'T OVERDO IT!

CHOP! CHOP!

GOBBLE GOBBLE GOBBLE

HOWWWL!

?

FUNNY SORT OF CREATURE!

LET'S FIND OUT WHAT IT TASTES LIKE. I'LL CATCH IT WHILE YOU LIGHT THE FIRE!

HEY, ASTERIX!

THAT GOBBLER HAS LOTS OF FRIENDS. WE'LL HAVE SOMETHING TO EAT WHILE WE WAIT FOR THE BOARS TO TURN UP.

GRRR! WOOF!

LET'S HOPE IT'S EDIBLE.

SOON AFTERWARDS...

IT'S GOOD!

YES, BUT IT MIGHT BE EVEN BETTER STUFFED... SCRUNCH!... WITH BOAR, FOR INSTANCE...

SCRUNCH! SCRUNCH!

GRRRR!

TALK OF THE DEVIL... THERE MUST BE A BOAR OVER THERE. I'LL GO AFTER IT. WE CAN USE IT TO STUFF THE THIRD GOBBLER.

BE CAREFUL!

JUST LOOK AT THIS!

???

20

I'M GOING TO TEACH YOU A HUNTSMAN'S TRICK! YOU IMITATE THE CRY OF YOUR QUARRY. LISTEN!

GOBBLE GOBBLE GOBBLE! GOBBLE!

GOBBLE GOBBLE GOBBLE!

OVER IN THAT TREE ... OF COURSE, THOSE GOBBLERS ARE BIRDS, SO THEY MUST HAVE NESTS. THAT'S THE DIFFERENCE BETWEEN GOBBLERS AND BOARS.

YES, I CAN SEE ITS FEATHERS! NOW TO GET HOLD OF IT!

TWEET, TWEET, TWEET ...

?!

KERPLONK!

IT'S A ROMAN DISGUISED AS A GOBBLER ... WE CAN'T EAT HIM, BUT HE CAN TELL US THE WAY TO THE VILLAGE!

LOOK, ASTERIX! JULIUS CAESAR HAS STARTED DISGUISING HIS LEGIONARIES AS GOBBLERS! THESE ROMANS ARE ...

ASTERIX?

LET'S SEE... ASTERIX NEVER TAKES HIS HELMET OFF EXCEPT TO EAT AND SLEEP...

... AND HE WASN'T EATING, BECAUSE HE WAS WAITING FOR ME AND THE GOBBLERS, AND IF HE WAS ASLEEP HE'D BE HERE... SO SOMETHING MUST HAVE HAPPENED TO HIM.

?!?

PAF!

YOU, ROMAN! WHERE'S ASTERIX?

ASTERIX WOULD KNOW HOW TO MAKE HIM TALK... SO FIRST I MUST FIND ASTERIX!

POF!

SEEK! SEEK, DOGMATIX!

SNIFF! SNIFF!

I THINK HE'S CHALLENGING YOU!

YOU DO?

GLUG! GLUG!

PAF!

I'VE FINISHED MINE.

MY TURN, THEN.

TCHAC!

PAFFF!

HOHOHOHOHOHOHOHOH

SOON AFTERWARDS...

I THINK HE WANTS US TO STAY HERE.

LOOK, I'M NOT JOINING UP IN THE ROMAN ARMY!

WELL, LET'S ACCEPT. THAT WAY WE MAY FINALLY FIND OUT WHERE WE ARE.

A LITTLE LATER...

LET HIM. IT MUST MEAN WE'VE BEEN TAKEN ON AS RECRUITS.

WHO'D HAVE THOUGHT I'D EVER WEAR THE UNIFORM OF A ROMAN MERCENARY?

HAVE YOU NOTICED THE LITTLE CRETAN GIRLS? I WOULDN'T MIND BEING IN THIS CRETE WITH A FEW LIKE THAT...

WELL, DON'T GO BEING INDISCREET HERE.

GOBBLE GOBBLE?

WOOF WOOF.

SLAP!

SCRUNCH!

I'D LIKE TO KEEP THIS AS A SOUVENIR OF OUR DAY'S HUNTING...

ESPECIALLY AS THE IBERIANS SEEMED QUITE IMPRESSED WITH OUR TECHNIQUE!

UGH!

OH, HOW KIND!

?

AHU!

??

GRRRR!

I THINK IT'S HIS DAUGHTER, AND HE'S PLEASED SHE LIKES YOU.

WHAT?!

BONK!

HEY, THIS FAT IBERIAN GIRL IS FOLLOWING ME AROUND!

GRRRR!

UGH!

TEE HEE HEE!

?

OLÉ!

WHAT DOES THAT CENTURION WANT ME TO DO?

I THINK HE WANTS YOU TO MARRY HIS DAUGHTER!

NO, THANK YOU VERY MUCH! I DON'T WANT TO BE A CENTURION'S SON-IN-LAW!

ANYWAY, I'M TOO YOUNG!

I THINK THE TIME HAS COME FOR US TO START LOOKING FOR OUR VILLAGE AGAIN... I'VE AN IDEA WE'RE A LONG WAY FROM HOME.

WHILE WE WERE HUNTING, I NOTICED THAT WE'RE ON AN ISLAND... WE'LL NEED A BOAT.

I SAW SOME BOATS DOWN BY THE RIVER.

GOOD. TONIGHT WE'LL TRY TO WELSH ON OUR HOSTS!

TWO WELSH? WHAT, WITH ALL THESE CRETANS AND IBERIANS AROUND THE PLACE ALREADY?

31

MÅYBE HUNTINGSEÅSSEN HÅS SCENTED LÅND...

PAT! PAT! PAT! PAT!

WHÅT LÅND, HERENDETHELESSEN?

I DØN'T BELIEVE IN THIS LÅND YØU KEEP ØN ABØUT! NØ ØNE BELIEVES IN IT! THERE ISN'T ÅNY LÅND! WE'RE GØING TØ CØME TØ THE EDGE ØF THE SEÅ AND THEN FÅLL ØFF, BY THØR!

YØU NEVER BELIEVE ÅNYTHING, STEPTØANSSEN! I'M SURE THERE'S LÅND ÅHEAD! IT MÅY EVEN BE INHÅBITED!

I SHÅLL DISCØVER THIS LÅND, ÅND TÅKE HØME SØME ØF THE NÅTIVES TØ PRØVE IT!

LET'S TURN BÅCK WHILE THERE'S STILL TIME! WHÅT DØ YØU SÅY, HÅRÅLDWILSSEN? ÅND YØU, NØGØØDREÅSSEN? ÅND YØU LØT?

YERSSE!

GRØØ....AAARR!

THÅT HØUND ØF YØURS IS BEGINNING TØ ...

LØØK! LØØK, BY ØDIN!

34

WOOF! WOOF!

A SHIP!

ROMAN, GOTHIC, EGYPTIAN OR WHAT?

WHO CARES? THAT SHIP MAY BE ABLE TO GET US HOME!

THOSE MERCENARIES MIGHT WELL CATCH UP WITH US... AND THEY WOULDN'T BE VERY PLEASED WE GOT AWAY... SPECIALLY YOU!

HOW RIGHT YOU ARE! LET'S SIGNAL TO THEM!

3/A

SOON AFTERWARDS,

I'VE BUILT A LITTLE HEAP OF STONES... BUT DO YOU REALLY THINK...

YOU WANT TO MARRY THE CENTURION'S DAUGHTER?

NO FEAR! I VALUE MY LIBERTY!

WELL THEN...

3/B

36

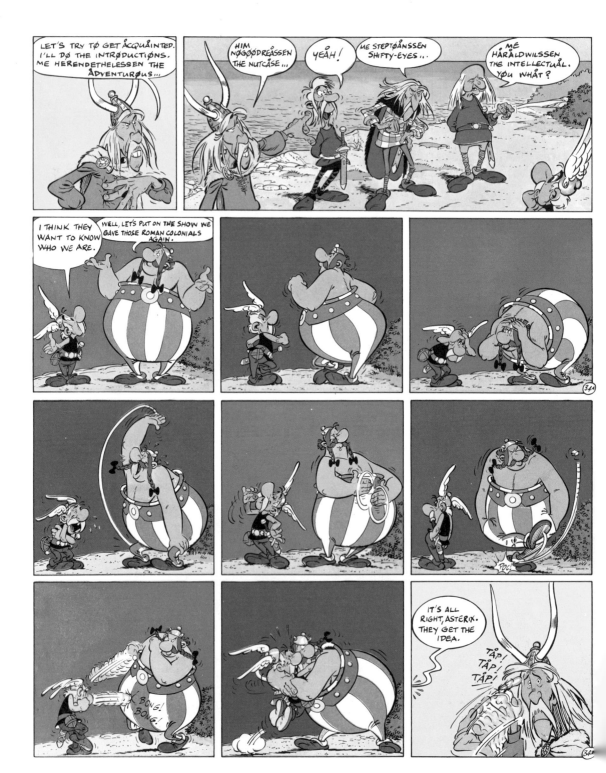

SURE ENOUGH, IT IS A FAST CROSSING, AND SOON A THICK FOG COVERS THE ICY SEA...

LÅND!

WE'RE BÅCK! PREPÅRE TØ HÅVE HØNØURS HEÅPED UPØN YØU!

ØH, THERE YØU ÅRE ÅT LÅST, HERENDETHELESSEN! YØU LÅZY BLIGHTER! BY ØDIN, WHERE THE NIFLHEIM HÅVE YØU BEEN?

IT'S... IT'S ØDIUSCØMPÅRISSEN THE TERRIFYING, THE CHIEF ØF ØUR TRIBE!

ØF CØURSE IT'S ØDIUSCØMPÅRISSEN! DID YØU THINK IT WÅS Å DEÅR LITTLE MERMÅID?

I SÅLUTE YØU, Ø CHIEF ØDIUSCØMPÅRISSEN!

ÅND I DØN'T SÅLUTE YØU!

WHILE WE WERE ÅLL ØUT ØN Å RÅIDING EXPEDITIØN, MR HERENDETHELESSEN WENT FØR Å CRUISE!

WE HÅVE PILLÅGED ÅND BURNT, WE'VE BRØUGHT BÅCK PLUNDER, SLÅVES, WHILE YØU...

WHILE I'VE BEEN DISCØVERING Å WØRLD... Å NEW WØRLD!

41

WAIT A MOMENT! WHO ARE YOU, AND WHAT ARE YOU DOING HERE?

I'M A GAUL, LIKE YOU. MY NAME IS CATASTROFIX ...

I'M A FISHERMAN. I WAS UNLUCKY ENOUGH TO RUN INTO SOME VIKINGS OUT ON A RAID ... THEY CAPTURED ME, BUT YOU HAVE SAVED MY LIFE!

WE MUST ESCAPE WHILE THEY'RE BUSY FIGHTING. THEY ARE VERY CRUEL. THEY WANT TO SACRIFICE YOU TO THEIR GODS!

THESE VIKINGS ARE CRAZY!

TAP! TAP!

DO YOU KNOW HOW WE CAN GET BACK TO GAUL?

YOU BET! THEY CAPTURED MY BOAT TOO ... IT'S TIED UP OVER THERE.

LOOK, THEY'VE EVEN LEFT MY NET IN IT!

GREAT! WE'LL BE ASKING YOU A FAVOUR ON THE WAY HOME ...

IF HE TELLS YOU TO THROW OUT YOUR NET, WATCH IT!

OH, LAY OFF IT, CAN'T YOU?

?

THE GAULS! WHERE ARE THEY?

46

47

THE END